Why We'll *Never*
Understand Each Other

Other Non Sequitur Books by Wiley

The Non Sequitur Survival Guide for the Nineties

Non Sequitur's Beastly Things

The Legal Lampoon:
A Biased, Unfair, and Completely Accurate Law Review from Non Sequitur

Why We'll *Never* Understand Each Other

By Wiley Miller

Andrews McMeel Publishing

Kansas City

Non Sequitur is distributed internationally by Universal Press Syndicate.

Why We'll Never Understand Each Other copyright © 2003 by Wiley Miller. All rights reserved. Printed in the United States of America. No part of this book may be used or reproduced in any manner whatsoever without written permission except in the case of reprints in the context of reviews. For information, write Andrews McMeel Publishing, an Andrews McMeel Universal company, 4520 Main Street, Kansas City, Missouri 64111.

03 04 05 06 07 BBG 10 9 8 7 6 5 4 3 2 1

ISBN: 0-7407-3387-7

Library of Congress Control Number: 2002113729

www.uComics.com

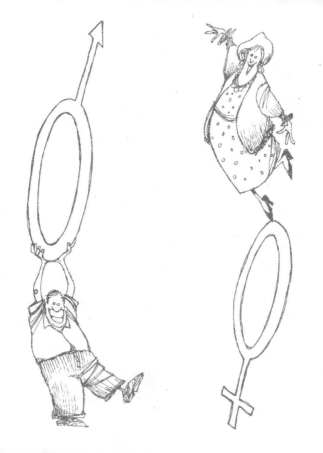

6

Seriousness is the only refuge of the shallow.
Oscar Wilde (1854-1900)

Here we are at the peak of the information age. We can communicate instantly with virtually anyone around the globe and, with just a few keystrokes and Internet access, we have the sum of our collected knowledge literally at our fingertips. We've figured out the inner structure of the atom and the creation of outer space, despite the fact that we've never been able to actually see them. We even have a pretty good idea about the social structure of dinosaurs based on fossilized bones that are over two hundred million years old.

Yet we are utterly clueless about how the person sleeping next to us thinks.

It seems we're born ignorant and only get progressively stupid as we try to figure each other out. And the harder we try, the more stupid we seem to get.

Perhaps we're just the butt of Nature's great cosmic joke.

The Dawn of Cluelessness
We begin our angst-ridden journey of unenlightenment
at the scene of the most pathetic and prolonged
mating ritual in all the animal kingdom: the singles' bar.

Like most mating rituals,
the singles' bar is predominantly
the male domain, in which the goal is
to lure eligible, and gullible, females inside.

Fortunately for women,
men aren't very imaginative at this.

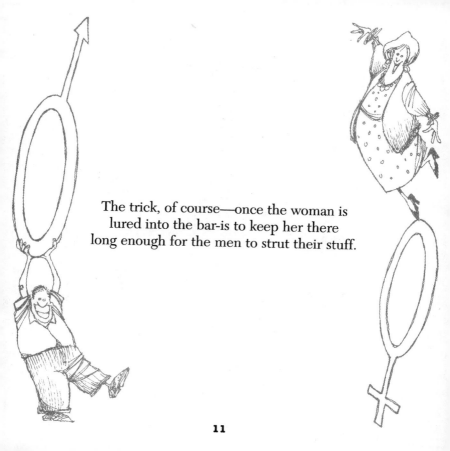

The trick, of course—once the woman is lured into the bar-is to keep her there long enough for the men to strut their stuff.

WHY PSYCHICS DON'T LINGER IN SINGLES BARS

This is the point when the fun begins,
as communication between the sexes stops.
Something odd happens to the words as they float from
our mouths, enter the ear of another and are interpreted
by their brain. Same species, different wiring.

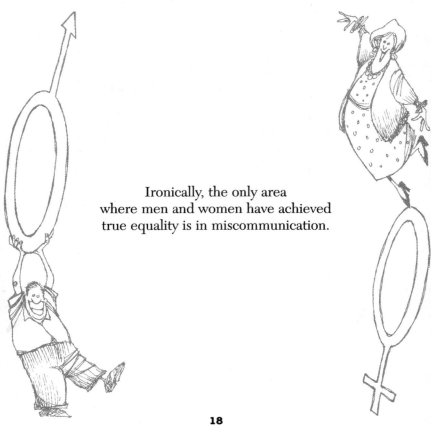

Ironically, the only area
where men and women have achieved
true equality is in miscommunication.

19

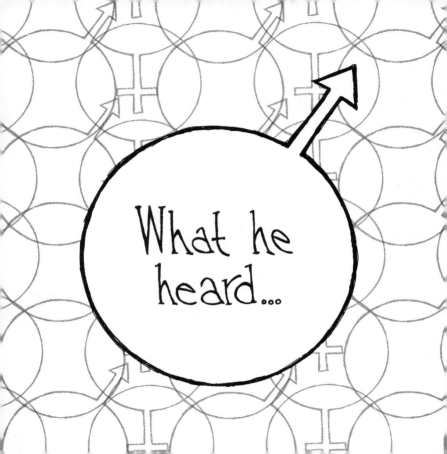

21

23

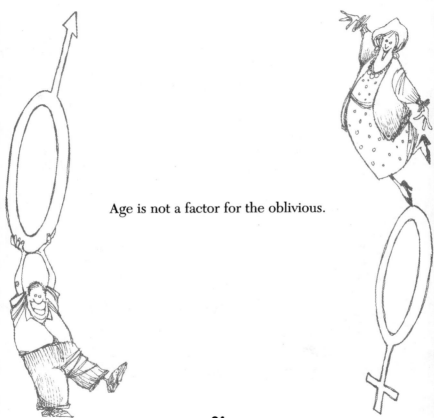

Age is not a factor for the oblivious.

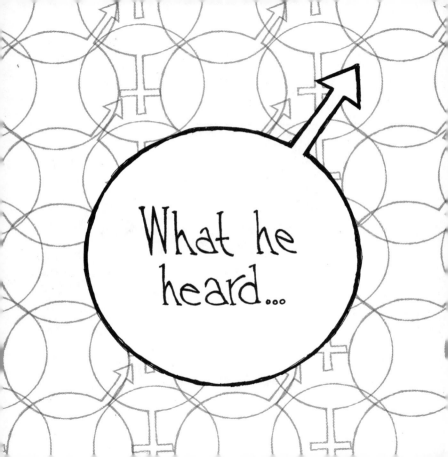

27

Perhaps our failure to understand each other
stems from our goals.

Men think short-term...

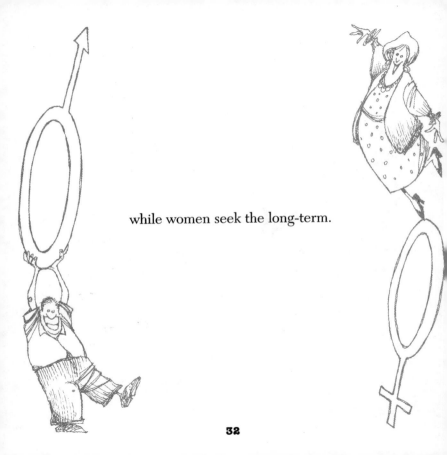

while women seek the long-term.

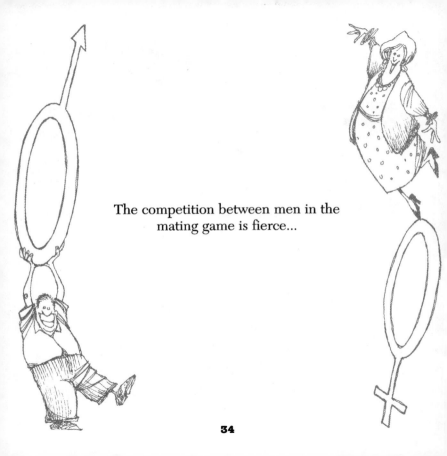

The competition between men in the
mating game is fierce...

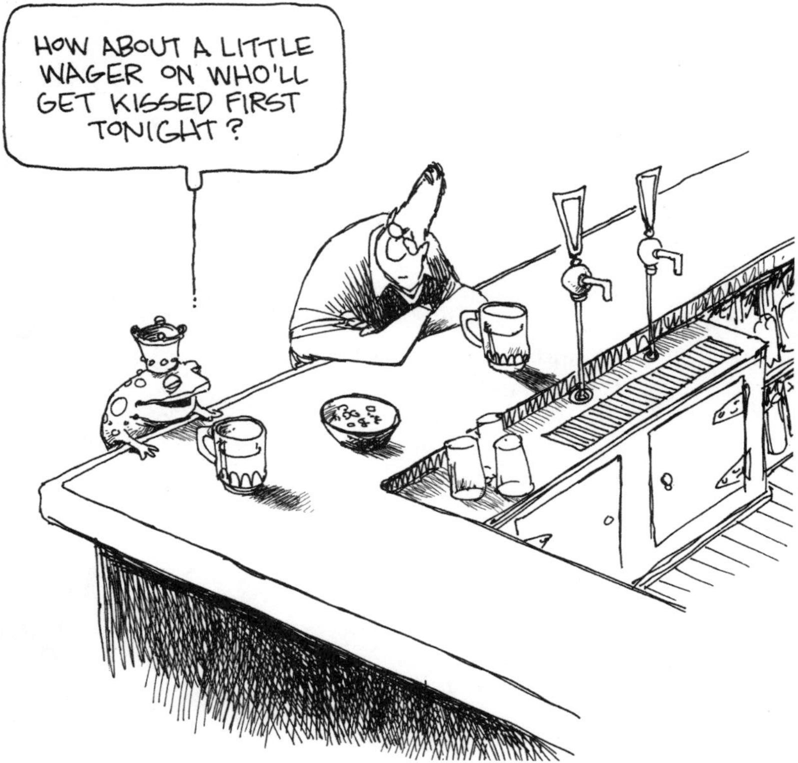
HOW ABOUT A LITTLE WAGER ON WHO'LL GET KISSED FIRST TONIGHT?

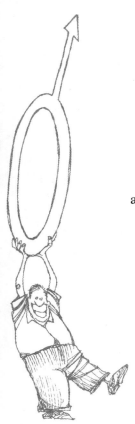

and carries on far beyond the
usual playing field.

37

Despite all our blunders,
we somehow manage to make a connection.
But fearing the worst,
we still approach with caution.

41

Once we've gotten over the seemingly
insurmountable hurdle of meeting someone,
we enter the next level of miscommunication: dating.

WHY CONTRACT LAWYERS
RARELY HAVE A SECOND DATE

WHEN DATING GOES FROM CASUAL TO SERIOUS...

43

The dating process, however, is done
on a strict trial-and-error basis.
And the rules are as firm as Jell-O.

46

As a relationship progresses,
we fool ourselves into thinking that
we really know each other
and begin to plunge headlong toward
a commitment.

This often leads to a premature celebration...

as reality begins to set in.

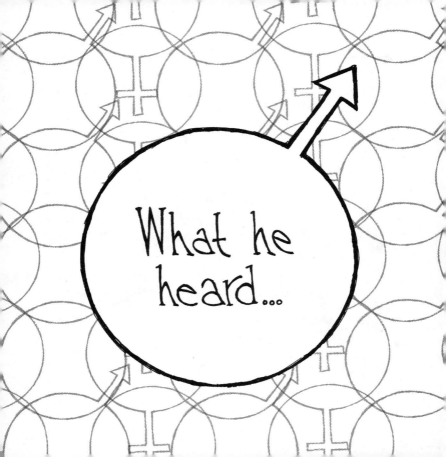

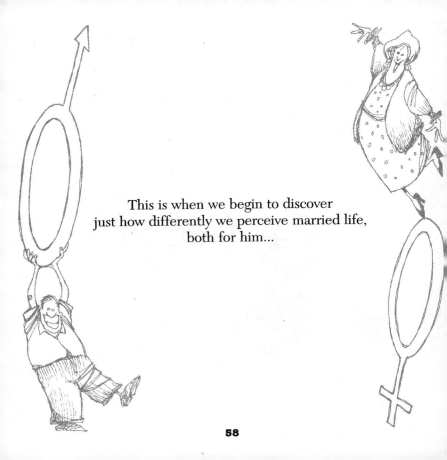

This is when we begin to discover
just how differently we perceive married life,
both for him...

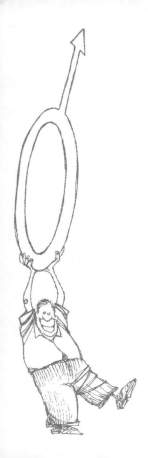

and for her.

60

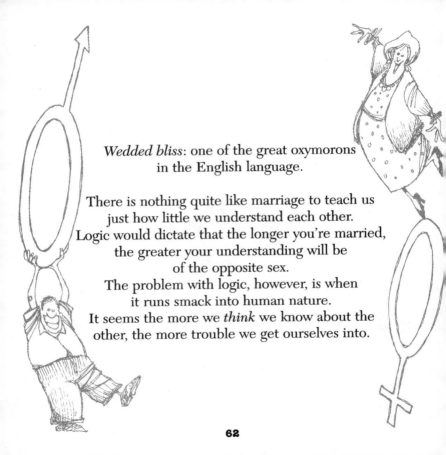

Wedded bliss: one of the great oxymorons
in the English language.

There is nothing quite like marriage to teach us
just how little we understand each other.
Logic would dictate that the longer you're married,
the greater your understanding will be
of the opposite sex.
The problem with logic, however, is when
it runs smack into human nature.
It seems the more we *think* we know about the
other, the more trouble we get ourselves into.

74

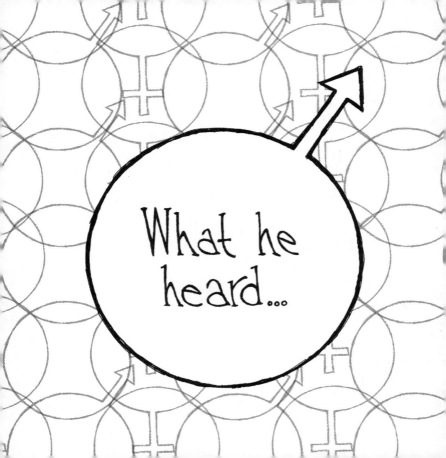

83

84

CRUEL *and* ALL TOO USUAL PUNISHMENT

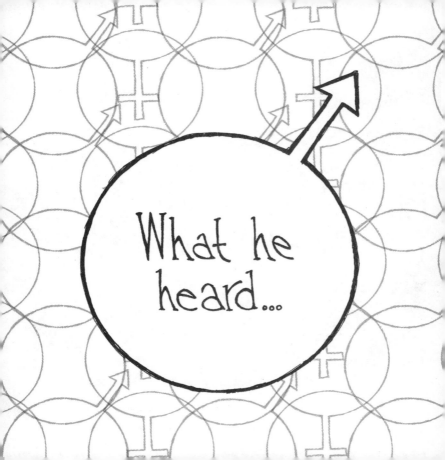

87

90

91

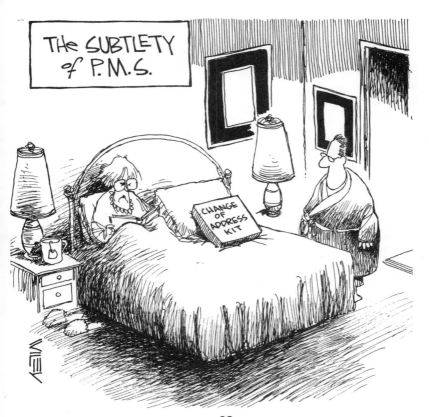

93

95

97

99

WHY MOST SUPERHEROES STAY SINGLE

103

A TALENT IN SEARCH of a NEED...

111

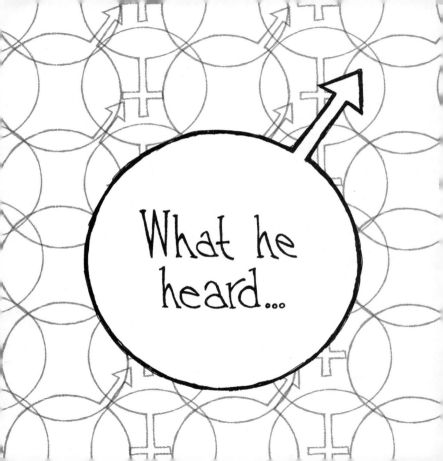

115

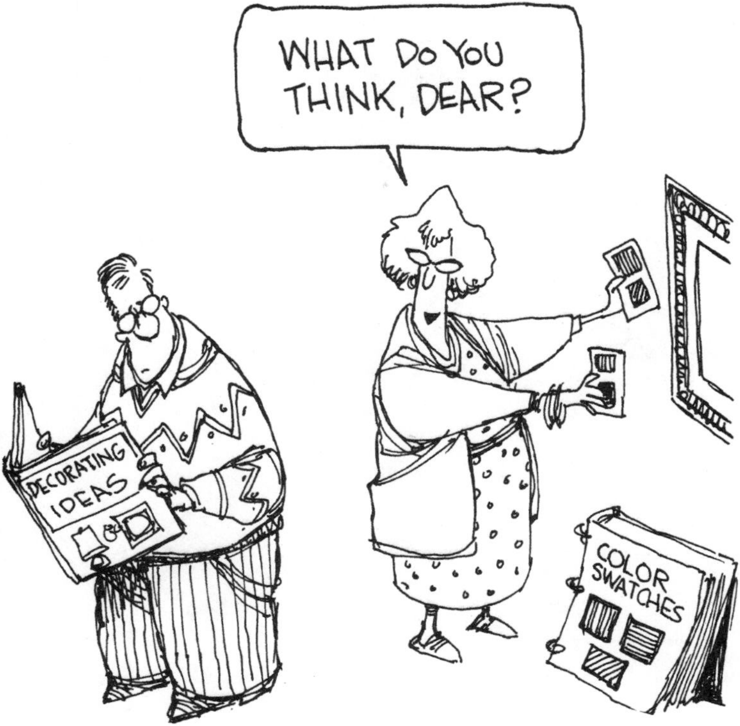
WHAT DO YOU THINK, DEAR?
DECORATING IDEAS
COLOR SWATCHES

THE SETTING OF A NEW LEGAL STANDARD FOR ASSISTED SUICIDE

119

125

THE OPTIMIST'S SPIN ON P.M.S.

131

Fairy tales always end with
"and they lived happily ever after."
Hardly a good way to prepare children
for the realities of adulthood, is it?

BRIDGING THE COMMUNICATIONS GAP...

137

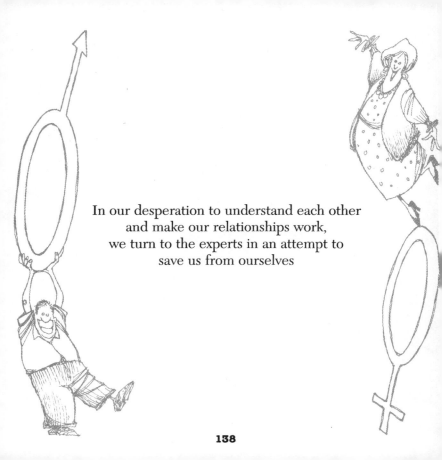

In our desperation to understand each other
and make our relationships work,
we turn to the experts in an attempt to
save us from ourselves

139

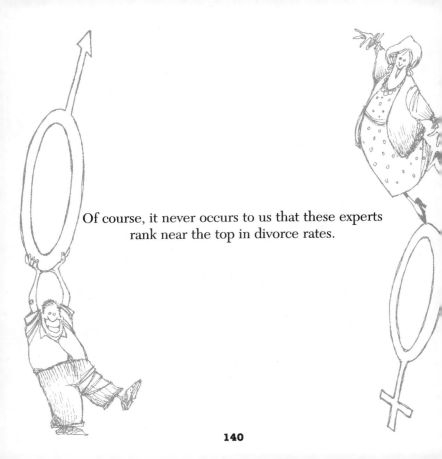

Of course, it never occurs to us that these experts rank near the top in divorce rates.

MY KEEN SENSE OF READING BODY LANGUAGE TELLS ME THAT YOU MIGHT ALREADY HAVE ONE FOOT OUT THE DOOR OF THE RELATIONSHIP, MIRIAM...
MARRIAGE COUNSELING

So we turn to another set of experts
and start all over again.

Is it all hopeless? No. We need only to
follow the lead of the French who do what
comes naturally to them: surrender.
Under their mantra of vive la différence, the
French have simply accepted the fact that we'll
never understand each other and wisely
advise us to just give in and go along for the ride.
And it's a ride that can't be topped
by any roller coaster.
All you can do is smile, hang on to each other
and scream.

143